THE RELUC+ANT MUM

The Reluc+ant Mum
Copyright © Maryann Laurence 2019 All Rights Reserved

The rights of Maryann Laurence to be identified as the author of this work have been asserted in accordance with the Copyright, Designs and Patents Act 1988

Spiderwize
Remus House
Coltsfoot Drive
Woodston
Peterborough
PE2 9BF

www.spiderwize.com

A CIP catalogue record for this book is available from the British Library.

The views expressed in this work are solely those of the author and do not necessarily reflect the views of the publisher, and the publisher hereby disclaims any responsibility for them.

ISBN: 978-1-912694-84-6

eBook ISBN: 978-1-912694-85-3

THE RELUC+ANT MUM

MARYANN LAURENCE

SPIDERWIZE
Peterborough UK
2019

*Dedicated with love to those I call family
without you my life would be empty.
xxx*

*And to Kate for being my
friend down the years xx*

Some names and places have been altered.

The four books make up -

FOUR SEASONS IN SALLY'S LIFE.

In reading order, they are -

THE RELUC+ANT MUM

IT'S POSITIVE: TAKE TWO

THE DARK TUNNEL I WALKED DOWN

IT'S LIKE THE MARRIAGE NEVER HAPPENED

If you want to read further on any of the issues covered in the books, please feel free to visit my website. I have a help page that has links to click on – the links take you outside of my webpage and could offer advice and opinions that differ to mine.

www. folded-corner.weebly.com

Season One - It all starts here

Something old

Something new

Something borrowed

Something blue!

24th April - Spring in North West England. Well, what can I say about that? A little rain, a little sunshine and not too cold; out for a walk, taking in the views of Windermere with my fiancé Ian, planning our wedding. Work is fine, the relationship is going well, life is good.

As for the wedding it's almost a year away and there's so many dreamy things to arrange, my head's in a whirl!

30th April - We visited Ian's grandmother, she lives on the very edge of town, she's 94 and as vibrant as ever! But I couldn't concentrate on the visit, I've been feeling very strange recently, I'm very emotional, and my mood doesn't so much swing as swish! My period is due in a couple of days – joy oh joy! Sore boobs, swollen abdomen, snappy attitude, the lot!

7th May - This is very odd, nothing has happened 'down below', no signs at all. Oh well, my last few 'monthlies' were very light and my GP is of the opinion I may not be ovulating so a missed period could be normal. But I don't feel normal. I'm very tearful, and I think I felt a little queasy this morning!

Now now girl, don't get any rash thoughts.

It can't be.

No.

Don't even think about it.

NO! NO! NO!

10th May - I met with Ian at lunchtime and we had a very serious chat sitting on the bench overlooking the lake, then we went to the chemist and I bought a home pregnancy testing kit. I'm screaming on the inside, I'm not sure I can handle the thoughts racing around my mind. I'll do the test in the morning at home; it's Ian's birthday tomorrow, it'll certainly make an original present that's for sure! Don't panic, the Doctor must be right, I'll bet I'm just not ovulating, **I can't be pregnant.**

11th May - I woke with the lark at 5.30am and went to the bathroom to do the test.

!! OH MY DAYS IT'S POSITIVE !!

I try to visualise greeting Ian at lunchtime 'Happy birthday, you're going to be a daddy!' The instructions said to 'leave the test to stand for 3 minutes to allow it to take effect and change colour'. Three minutes ... no, it didn't take that long for the two windows to turn blue! I kept going back to the bathroom over the next half an hour to see if it had changed its mind and gone back to clear. But no. It's there. The evidence is before my eyes, it's blue, it's positive, I'm pregnant. I'd like to cry but I'm so mixed up and in shock I can't do anything as sensible as cry. I made myself a drink and sat down before getting ready for work, and all the time trying to think of what to say when I see Ian at lunchtime.

I put 'the result' in a waterproof cover and wrapped it in birthday paper to give him. Well, what else could I do? Just how are you supposed to break this kind of news to your fiancé on their birthday?

Lunchtime. Due to the shape of the test Ian thought the present was a pen. He lifted it out gingerly and looked at it. It's obviously not a pen now it's in the light of day. His expression was confusion, and then shock. "What does this mean? Is this? Are you?" "Yes, It's positive, I'm pregnant." And that was all the conversation we could manage. He kept saying "Wow" over and over and gazing into space. To be honest, I was hoping for a bit more ... something or other.

OK, it may have been a sneaky way to break it to him, but I couldn't think of anything else. The next thing was to tell his parents, we didn't want them hearing it on the gossip hot line. So we went to their house after work and announced the news. Ian told them - well, they are his parents - I'll telephone my sister. Reaction from his mum – "Oh, well, congratulations" and she gave me a sort of peck on the cheek. Reaction from his dad – he did not speak to us for the next 15 days until **he'd** got used to the idea!

That evening we went out for a meal with friends to

celebrate Ian's birthday, and after everyone had eaten we told them the news - we thought we'd leave it till after the meal as the news might have put some of them off eating. Some were very pleased and happy for us, some though, were clearly not!

Later, when I was home alone, I sat and took time to think and to consider my options. As far as I could see they were –

1.   Keep the baby and face the consequences

2.   Adoption

3.   Abortion

These were the only ones I could think of, I was in such a state of panic and I wanted to try to understand how each one would affect me.

Option one - I would have my life changed forever.

Option two - I would have the baby but not raise it myself.

Option three - I would be able to keep my life as it is – my house, holidays, car and etc.

I took a moment to think, but in truth it wasn't long. I found I couldn't go through with option three. And having carried the baby and given birth I truly believe I wouldn't want to hand the baby over. So, it's option one then – despite all the changes it would mean, I'm unexpectedly pregnant, carrying an unplanned baby, and what's more I'm going to keep the baby and raise it. WOW! I need a lie down!

16th May - Appointment at the doctors. I remembered to collect an early morning sample of pee and saw my GP. I found filling in forms took up more time than I spent with my GP, and he didn't even test my sample! I decided on the hospital where I'll give birth, was issued with a certificate for free prescriptions and got told the estimated due date – January 12th, then I went into work where all the girls were very happy for me.

But why wasn't I happy?

The next day I had a conversation with Ian about us getting married after the baby had arrived, but he wouldn't hear of it, he wants us to be married before the baby's arrival and before I have too much of a pregnancy bump! So...

... the rest of the week was a blur. The wedding was moved to take place in 9 weeks' time (nine solitary weeks to arrange a wedding!). Chapel and reception date changed, dresses organised, food, shoes, hair-dressers, suits, best man, bridesmaids, my maid of honour was being flown in, flowers, seating arrangements, order of service, wedding practice, invitations, band for the evening ceilidh, cake, decorations for Chapel's hall, photographer, DVD. Phew! Somehow, it was all happening.

It was happening all right, and it was happening *very* fast.

But why don't I get all gooey and coo and ooh when I talk about the baby, or when I see babies in the street, or why don't I get excited when I see an expectant-mum with an expectant-tum waddle down the street? Why oh why? What's happening to me? What's happening to my body?

Morning sickness - never suffered with it. Cravings? No not me. We invented one – apple pie, custard, ice-cream and a flake or two!

But is it supposed to be like this? Do other women go through this uncertainty when facing an unplanned pregnancy? I keep wanting to cry.

Some people are just hearing the news and are coming out with 'Oh you must be so happy'. Must I? Why? What's there to be happy about? My life has just been turned upside down by something no bigger than a pin head.

2nd June - we're trying to lead a near-normal life. Ian's moved in to my house to look after me, to make sure I don't carry anything too heavy or fall down the stairs. Some of our friends are being very supportive, some are definitely not, I'm trying to avoid those ones! I bumped into a friend of mine at a concert the other evening and told him my news, he was definitely unimpressed! Seeing such obvious disappointment on his face made me dreadfully sad. I hid this from everyone. I never told anyone how I was truly feeling because I didn't think they'd believe me, and in truth no one was really interested in me, it seemed they were only interested in the baby. Plus some folk had opinions they had to tell me, such as what I should and shouldn't be eating and drinking and doing and not doing – do they think I've turned into some sort of imbecile that doesn't know what's what about eating and drinking when you're pregnant! I know I'm a novice but I'm not bloody stupid.

One thing that has completely taken me by surprise though, is the change to my driving and it happened overnight, I've become a very careful and considerate driver – and it's because I now have another life I'm personally responsible for. I like it, because before I got pregnant I was a bit irrational and a bit unthinking, but all of that has gone now, and despite all my confusion and uncertainty, the thought of being a responsible parent is very strong, and there's no doubt about it, it's here to stay.

9th June - After a few rounds of visiting the midwife the whole thing is confirmed at the hospital by a scan. There is a very strong heartbeat. I'm starting to feel quite maternal... this lasts about a week.

18th June - I've got quite a pronounced 'bump' and am getting asked 'Is it twins?' My thoughts take a leap from panic to extreme fear. TWINS? I really hope it's not. We visit Ian's parents and they tell us of copious amounts of twins on their side of the family, and after visiting a couple of my cousins (on both sides of my family) I get told of twins all over the family tree. This thought fills me with sheer horror.

I remember my mum telling me that when she was pregnant with me that her bump was so large she'd only go outside when it was dark (this still makes me smile). I'm miss mum and dad very much, but, now I'm pregnant, I miss my mum. I don't get on with Ian's parents, not really, this makes me feel sad and lonely – isolated almost – but I've not said anything as I've not got anyone around to talk to about stuff like this. I don't think anyone would understand what I'm going through, and sadly no one asks.

The wedding now looms nearer, Lily, one of my bridesmaids is making all the dresses, but I have to confess I fear my waistline may not fit into my beautiful dress. Lily and Rosalyn my bridesmaids as well as Helen my maid of honour are amongst the few friends I have supporting me – shining stars in this confusing journey called pregnancy and marriage.

Wedding lists! There's lists upon lists being made and none seem to be getting any shorter.

What is happening to my body? It doesn't seem to belong to me anymore. I'm becoming a vessel, not a person.

The next thing Ian does is drag me away - almost screaming and kicking - for a weekend visiting his friends Karl and Vicky in York! I'm not ok with this as I've never met them, and actually I can't go away! Not for a whole weekend, I have things to do, people to see, a wedding to organise! What happened to our near normal life? I drove us to York as my stress levels were through the roof – it poured with rain for the whole journey, it took hours to get there and Ian was asleep; I sang softly to myself so as not to wake him, and to keep my nerves company.

The weekend was OK I guess. We all went on walks, sat and watched movies, ate pizza, relaxed and unwound. But I felt I couldn't discuss anything with them as I don't know them well – besides they were too busy talking to Ian, and between the three of them they organised and arranged the honeymoon!

One place we did go to was the Edinburgh Wool Shop and looked at the lovely jumpers. Ian was looking at the men's Aran jumpers and said he'd like one but they're a bit pricey, so I decided to knit him one in secret and give it to him as a surprise present. We came home to face the time left before the wedding.

The next few weeks flew by. I didn't have a hen night due to being pregnant, and the night before the wedding I was home alone and had a quiet night in, apart from going to get fish and chips. I told the man in the chippy that I was getting married the following day and he said 'Congratulations' but then he commented that I didn't look very happy, I told him it was nerves. I was trying to hide my thoughts about the wedding. At home I sat and reflected on how my life had changed in such a short time. Here I was with an unplanned pregnancy and getting married tomorrow. The thing is, I'm not sure I should be going ahead with it. And the only person I've got for company this evening is me. So, I tried the fors and againsts.

For – getting married	Against – getting married
I'm pregnant.	I'm not sure I love Ian enough for it to last for a 'life time'.
No other reason.	I'm not sure he is the right man for me.
Can't think of anything else.	I'm not sure .....

Oh dear.

It's nearly 11.30pm as I climb the stairs to bed, I'm really very tired, I think I'm going ahead with the wedding, but I have to admit the fors and againsts list keeps playing on my mind.

Once in the bedroom, I look around and see my beautiful dress is ready, together with the veil, shoes and blue garter – oh great, the last time I saw anything blue was my pregnancy test! Hmmm not really the right attitude. Time for sleep, I'm getting married tomorrow.

Wedding Day! - Mid morning my two bridesmaids, Lily and Rosalyn, turned up and we went to the hairdressers in town; it was a lovely sunny day and we went by train. We were laughing and joking about what I'd do if someone spoke out when the Pastor asks ...'if anyone knows of any reason why these two should not be married ....' We got home and had a light lunch, and that's when my maid of honour arrived, thank goodness for Helen, she sorted everyone out and got us all on track! The girls helped me into my dress in a sort of rota as there were so many buttons – we also giggled as the dress was a bit 'snug around the waist' than it had been previously! Baby 'bump' was obviously starting to grow.

We did our makeup and everyone was dressed and getting ready to leave the house. The girls went downstairs as the flowers and the cars had arrived; it was all starting to happen. I went downstairs to join them, but just as Helen was putting my head dress and veil in place the enormity of the day suddenly overwhelmed me and I stared deeply into her eyes, like a rabbit caught in the headlights. She saw my face and the look I was giving her, then she held up her hand to me (her palm towards me gesturing me to stop), and said 'Not now!', and off the girls went in one of the cars. This left me with Dennis Bamforth (a close friend and conductor of Manchester Recorder Orchestra, he was walking me down the aisle) plus Andrew, the driver of our car.

We left the house and the two of them managed to get me - and my dress - into the back of the car and off we set. On route to the Chapel I was staring at my flowers and went very quiet, I was still having thoughts about not going through with the wedding, I'm not sure if Ian is really the man for me. Dennis took my hand and asked me if I was ok, I feigned a smile and the journey (and the day) continued.

What made up my mind to go through with the wedding? Being pregnant.

It was a nice sunny day for a wedding (but why did it have to be mine?). An army of friends had done lots to make it a great day. My best friend Mij did the readings, my life long friend David was usher, and John and Rosamunde prepared all the food. It was lovely to have my friends with me.

Then we set off for a week honeymooning on the Isle of Lewis. This was ok except I had no interest in consummating the marriage – it took nearly the whole week before I ran out of excuses and gave in to him.

But of course 'bump' came with us. And bump was about to put in more of an appearance than had been showing previously. Taking it out of me if I walked too far, nudging me when I turned over in bed, cut out my drinking habit, changed my eating habit, pulling strangely when I swam and extracted me from my memory - has it gone forever?

Growing and growing. Why oh why didn't I *feel* anything towards my bump?

What did I expect to feel? Oh I don't know, love I suppose. Excitement. Desire to know what sex it is. What it looks like, who it looks like. If it will have this and that, and all the rest. But I don't. It just continues to grow, and I just continue...

Back home we settled into a pattern of life, with the round of sandwiches for lunch the next day, breakfast, catching the train for work into and home from the city for me, home, tea, shopping, swimming (not too much of this for me I'm afraid), visitors that turn up unexpectedly and won't go! More work, more shopping, less and less sleep.

This last one really has started to take its toll on me. Not only is my body getting used to being pregnant, but Ian snores and dreams noisily, and of course there are male 'night antics'.

10th August - and it's 'The Official Scan', we now have two photos, one that gets handed around and is already promoted to a 'framed picture' and one that's on the fridge. I get told that compared to some mums I'm really quite healthy. But do they go through all this uncertainty and confusion? And who is there to speak to anyway?

I will say one thing I'm impressed with is Emma's Diary, I'm finding it really informative... what my body is going through and what baby is going through... size and development of baby... plus freebies to send for, though I have heard that some mums don't like it. Oh well, I guess we're all different.

Then I talked to a couple of girlfriends who have had babies in the last 12 months or so. The conversations are horrific!! Stories about the injections, the cut, the stitches, the blood, the baby, the placenta, the no-sleep-from-here-on-in, the nappies, the feeding...

None of this endears me to my growing bump. Sleeping through the night is almost a dream. For one reason or another it only happens now and then, I feel I'm living in a twilight world.

24th August - A midwife visit and I have a list of questions connected to my (minor) ailments. It really does not help when she tells me I'm having a perfectly normal pregnancy. What is normal about being pregnant anyhow?

Ian has been reading a book I brought him, it's for

expectant fathers, and it doesn't help me when he also tells me I'm having a normal pregnancy! But he should know, he read it in the book!

He is being understanding. I am not. And it does me no good when his book (yes the one I bought him!) tells him I should have a supercharged sex-drive, this is not what I'm experiencing. Sex? You've got to be kidding!

3rd September - I feel OK about the baby. About the pregnancy, the backache, my growing waist line, about none of my clothes fitting me, about the fact that I've got stretch marks on my boobs, my legs and my bum. I'm going to have a baby! I'm feeling OK about it all. I tell Ian and as you can imagine he is pleased.

But it didn't last.

This phase started on Tuesday when I came out of morning prayers at Chapel and finished with an upswing in backache on Saturday evening.

I tell people how I'm feeling (when they ask) and I get 'It's normal' or 'You'll go through worse than this before the end' and then there's 'This is nothing, you wait for the birth', at this point some people even laugh. None of this does anything to help.

My nose feels constantly blocked, as if I'm about to have a massive nose bleed. My back feels as if I've been kicked by someone wearing clogs, turning over in bed is not easy; Ian brings me a hot water bottle when I ask him.

Getting the train into and out of the city for work is also taking its toll on me, because at the local station there are no stairs nor a lift, only a long ramp between the platform and street level. This is becoming very tiring and I often have to haul myself up by the hand rail to get up to street level. Ian has the car, as he starts work 30 minutes earlier than me.

I'm feeling depressed about the whole damn thing. Over lunch Ian said, 'You're not enjoying your pregnancy are you?', 'No' I said, and meant it. What is there to enjoy? Look at my body! Count the bloody stretch marks!

7th September - I've been having some dizzy spells and little lights before my eyes. Work has been rather hectic recently, and maybe I've been overdoing it. Also my ankles have been swelling, not much, but it's definitely there. A little visit to the doctors may be necessary if these symptoms carry on.

12th September - I've got to have a week's rest, due to low blood pressure (!), I thought your pressure only went up. (Am I being totally naive?) A week of rest was what the doctor ordered, so that's what followed. A week where I tried to do things but ended in a heap mid-afternoon totally exhausted and sleeping for a couple of hours. Putting my feet up and doing nothing seems to be what my body wants - not however what I would like, but I don't seem to have a say in the matter. This way of life is far from the active life I enjoyed only a few months ago!

Bump has taken to alternating between aerobics and break dancing! My tum occasionally looks as if there are two of them in there trying to get out (not by the usual route). Heartburn has arrived and seems to enjoy making my life a misery.

The other night I woke up with heartburn in my chest plus backache. I lay there in the dark thinking 'this is awful', and silent tears fell.

19th September - Back to the doctors and I go back to work, almost feeling like a sane and normal human being. Back to the rat race my GP would like to save me from.

We've been invited to a wedding reception so I decided to make myself a dress, it looks quite nice as I'm putting it together. Having never seen me sew before, Ian is surprised by my dressmaking skills. Then I try it on. Oh my goodness! It's like wearing a parachute! It's huge! I take it in a little at the sides and that seems to give it a little more shape, but not a lot. I decide to wear one of my 'preggy' dresses instead.

The other evening we met up with some friends that have two children; the little girl is about 2 years old and the baby boy about 3 months. I asked Mum how things were going, and I found myself having quite a frank conversation about breast-feeding and learned to my horror that the boy does not sleep through the night, and needs feeding every 3 hours. EVERY THREE HOURS! GREAT SCOTT!

I have another mid-wife appointment at the end of the week and I'm taking the whole day off and going looking at baby things, I think I'm getting into the thoughts of being a mum at last.

Planning towards the appointment with the midwife this week my questions are getting quite interesting, such as Rhesus incompatibility between myself and Ian, this is quite an important factor and one that is totally new to me as Ian and I are opposites, he's A positive and I'm A negative (A+ and A-). Apparently I've got to have an injection shortly after the birth because any further pregnancies (am I doing this again?) and my body will see the new baby as a foreign object and will get rid of it – and this doesn't happen with the first one ... I'm impressed!

A full night's sleep is something I long for, sleeping has become a joke. I now have a pillow for my head, the duvet tucked in behind my back (possibly a hot water bottle if Ian remembers) and a pillow for bump! Turning over during the night disrupts my sleep a lot ... then there's Ian's snoring, plus he gets out of bed 3 – 4 times a night for a wee, then there's his 'manly night antics'! Sharing a bed isn't all it's made out to be.

Baby is now on the move and bumping around quite a bit, feeling the baby move inside me is quite an experience. It's very strange feeling something (gently) kick you, I can see my tummy move! Occasionally the movement is more pronounced and you can 'see' baby bump about. The other evening one of my cats was gently resting across my bump and got 'kicked', he leapt across the room and the expression on his face was hilarious.

23rd September - Another visit with the midwife, and this time it's a bit different and slightly more exciting. She measures the bump(!) and then she puts a microphone thingy on my tum and hey-presto there is the heartbeat coming from the inside. It's amazing. I'd been told it was a rather indistinguishable whooshy sound, but no, it's there, strong and regular.

Rosalyn came over the other evening, (Ian had gone out with his pals), she had been on the lookout for more baby things, this time things in blue to balance the things she had already brought in pink. I put them with the other 'stuff', there's quite a lot of things gathering in the spare bedroom now, cot, pram, carry cot, a box for carrying 'things' around, a food warmer, a baby-carrying-thing (that looks rather like an octopus), 2 bags full of baby clothes and another one full of things for the cot. There are cuddly toys and a bouncy chair.

Ian goes swimming on Sunday afternoons, and one Sunday I found I had a little energy to spare, so I carefully moved all the items out of my study, so it can be turned into a nursery, and I moved all the baby items in there. I'd - gently - done a couple of hours moving stuff around when Ian came home. I was very pleased with how much I'd achieved and was hoping for a 'Wow you've worked hard here' but no. He was beside himself! I got told off for not having waited for him to be there to help move things. It seems I can't do anything right.

11th October - I would like to know what to do with my backache, it affects me all the time, lying down, sitting and walking. Ian says he wishes he could share what I'm going through, but that's not a lot of help.

Yesterday I hadn't felt the baby move much during the day and got quite concerned, so when Ian was home from work I told him; he told me I was making a fuss over nothing and wouldn't go anywhere until he'd washed, eaten his evening meal and changed his clothes.

At the hospital the midwife was lovely and very understanding. She set me up on the monitor and what happens next is that baby moved around more in that 30 - 40 minutes than during the whole of the day. Little performer! When baby turned I could hear the sound of bubbles rippling around, and the sound on the speaker reminded me of the noise made in those submarine programs. It was reassuring to hear that everything is ok with little baby. Ian was too busy chatting to the nurses to notice, telling them how he knew I was making a fuss. I just relaxed, safe in the knowledge that baby was ok.

The heartburn is enjoying itself immensely and the back pain is making my walk look rather like a lilting gait! Do other mums get like this? No one tells you that it can be miserable being pregnant. Well, actually, no one says anything *before* you get pregnant. Once you are though the truth starts to seep out.

I've decided to find out more about this pregnancy business to help my nerves and try to calm my fears of the birth. I take myself off to the library and got a book about being pregnant and the birth (a horror story!) and I've just read a chapter on what to do if the baby is coming quickly and you're still at home with no way of getting to hospital! The words are of calm and comfort, but my feelings about not being surrounded by people who know exactly what they are doing (plus lots of pain relief!) are panicking as usual.

16th October - Started the 'kick chart' today, otherwise known as a "foetal movement chart". It says 'Start at 9am and if you've not felt 10 movements by 6pm ring the hospital. Otherwise tick off the chart till you have 10 kicks and note the time down at the 10th kick.' My noted time... 12.20 little performer.

I'm into my last but one week of work, and I can't wait for Friday next week. I really feel in need of rest. Real rest. Not just the normal pattern that has evolved of bed/bathroom/bed/turnover/wake-up/try not to put a pillow to good use to stop Ian's snoring!/adjust pillows/sleep a bit/alarm goes off! Real rest. I've got mixed emotions about working these last couple of weeks, I honestly thought I could handle it. I thought I would be able to cope with the time leading up to the suggested leaving/giving up work date as I coped really well with the weeks before, but no. It's proving to be quite a struggle. Yesterday morning in sheer frustration of my own tiredness and stroppy attitude, I stood in the kitchen and screamed, Ian didn't really know what to say or do – no surprise there.

I've finished the pregnancy book I've been reading and am now trying to put together a list of things to ask at the hospital when I'm there in December. Such as how the hospital feels about episiotomy, breast-feeding and birth positions. Further details on Rhs incompatibility. Can I keep my baby with me? Gosh, I'm really getting into all of this.

Oh well, another midwife's visit in a couple of days - has it really been 4 weeks since the last one? I'm not sure if I'll have many questions for her this time, the midwives are really supportive; I wonder what she has in mind. I'll be into visits every 2 weeks next. And then... I don't want to think about the "and then" bit just yet.

I'm finding that reading and re-reading sections in the book that covers labour and birth is helping to take away a bit of fear from what I've discovered is quite a taboo subject – people don't go into detail when you ask them. But having a bit of knowledge I feel I'm more prepared for "when it starts to happen". I used to think that you had your first contraction and the baby was on the way, and before you knew it you would be holding a mucky bundle and people would be queuing to congratulate the dad, slap his shoulders and say 'Well done' and taking him out for a beer to celebrate all his hard work!

What I've found out is this - I'm to have practice contractions (called Braxton Hicks), and that I've probably been having them for some time, but as these are painless (?!) then I don't know I've been having them. I've also read that labour is in three parts, and that the first and second part of the labour could take up to 15 hours. So, have a bath, take a stroll, have a light snack, listen to some music. Take it easy, you could have a long wait ahead of you. Oh great!

You never know, it may be a false alarm, and could all go away in a couple of hours.

WHAT!?

After all that build up towards the possible suspected date of anticipated arrival, a false alarm, good grief!

24th October - Here we are at then, my last week at work. This is proving to be both scary and exciting all at the same time. For a start off my income will be virtually nil, that's the scary bit as Ian's salary isn't good, and the exciting bit is that I'll be able to rest lots and do lots of "things" around the house. Like decorating the nursery, moving things around for when baby puts in an appearance, and all things like that. But most of all resting.

We've started decorating the hall, stairs and landing. We went shopping on Saturday for decorating materials and it took us 5 hours going from one store to another as we were following the advice of a friend of Ian's! This decorating lark is not as lovely as the advertisers make it out to be – especially when you're pregnant!

Yesterday evening we went along to our first parent-craft session and heard a midwife talk for 2 hours on labour, childbirth and pain relief, it wasn't too bad but then she said she'll cover "complications" next week! This course is not proving to be as enthralling or exciting (or organised) as it could be. For instance, we should have been shown a DVD of "The Birth" but there was no DVD player – so sadly the DVD spent the rest of the evening sat on the desk, often referred to and affectionately patted, but it never came out of its case.

With the parent-craft group there's a planned visit to a labour ward at a local hospital where we will be shown around and have all the equipment explained to us. I hope no one is "in action" so to speak, as I'm not sure I could cope with it.

25th October - I have another antenatal visit with the midwife where "the bump" was measured, and we heard baby's heartbeat. I had a blood test and was weighed (this proved not too embarrassing) and was given a little card due to the Rhs incompatibility, and away I came. But this time she sees me out of the door with "I'll see you in two weeks' time". Two weeks? Has it come to that already? This time it's two weeks, and in a short while it'll be weekly visits (may be that should be spelt weakly!). This is another sign that the due date is getting closer. Another sign is that my navel, my nice neat "innie" is getting shallower. I'm hoping it will flatten out gracefully, but Ian argues, and is downright convinced, that it will stick out unceremoniously.

The clocks have gone back, and this is another step towards the "EDD". Then it will be Christmas - what a joy that'll be, waddling around and not being able to eat a reasonable sized meal due to the fact that my uterus will be where my stomach usually is, and my stomach will be elongated and squashed up under my bust line - joy oh joy! Then there's explaining to the world why we are not going around visiting as we did last year – some people are not being very understanding about this! And of course, Ian still thinks we should visit the world and his wife! No doubt we'll be expected to do the Christmas Day family meal thing at Ian's parents, there's no getting out of that one, not even if the world stopped turning!

Then it will be January....

The official date is the 12th, but of course baby could arrive 2 weeks either side of that date, so January it is - or should be at any rate if all goes ok; the date to be determined by a natural course of events. I think the uncertainty over the due date and the time when things will happen adds to my fears as I can't actually say when or how or where or be organised about anything to do with the actual event. I just have to wait for it to happen. This is not what I would like, but I have to be happy with what Mother Nature has planned. Baby will come when baby is ready, and not before. A matriarch aunt of mine believed that, if the baby was a boy, he won't come 'till his "Peter" is ready! I wonder what her excuse would be if it turned out to be a girl?

28th October - My last day of work. Baby has been bumping around more of late, and I've noticed an increase in activity if I get out of bed during the night (what do you mean "if"?) settling down again is proving difficult to say the least. The heartburn has increased, plus I'm getting cramp.

I'm not actually able to describe my feelings at the moment. Feelings such as relief due to not having to put up with the hustle and bustle of getting myself to work and standing on trains and buses; but then there's the nice thought of rest when I need it - and I really feel I need it some days - but then there's the fear of not having a salary credited to my bank account. Also, having been in work since leaving college I'm afraid I'll vegetate, and that when I try to return to work I'll find it more of a problem because I may have missed out on some new equipment / computer updates entering the work place, and of course I'll now be responsible for a baby - and what do I do if baby is ill? Who will look after baby when I'm at work, and how much will that cost me? There's a lot more to consider than I ever thought.

At parent-craft this week they showed us "The Birth" DVD, It was admittedly very informative, explaining about exercise, pain relief and positions as well as the importance of trying to keep mobile during the early stages of labour. And then came "the birth". This looked as painful as I had imagined. I felt the DVD was a bit misleading as it only showed a couple of snatches of the labour, birth and cleaning up process. I thought it gave a false sense of the time it all took. What amazed me was the speed at which the baby's body (and etc) was born after the slow delivery of the head. No sooner was the head pushed out, then with the next contraction (or two) splash! The baby was out and being cleaned up, then mum was cuddling and feeding the baby and her birth partner was looking on with awe, and the midwife was left to deal with the placenta and clean up the mess.

The DVD was helpful in its information about this and that, but I didn't want a ring side seat of a baby being born in the first place so I was never going to like that bit. I felt sorry for the woman in the DVD as it can't have been nice to have a camera pointing at her like that.

29th October - I take part in a concert with the orchestra I'm in, but my dilemma was over what to wear? My white blouse only just about fits, and as for my long black skirt, it will only zip up half way. So I wore a longer blouse, and I then used a rubber band hooked from the button hole to the button. The concert went well and I put my orchestra clothes away.

30th October - Parent-craft. This was the visit to a local hospital, going around the labour ward and delivery suite. Learning in the process that, as I am a 'mature mum', the school-given polio drops have probably worn off and that I need to request a polio drop when baby has one. The delivery suite was exceedingly hot and more than one mum-to-be crossed their legs when shown a board that had holes drilled in it that represent the size you dilate to when you are in labour. This is not a nice prospect - 10cm is a lot when you don't normally have any "cm" at all. Fortunately, the labour ward was having a quiet evening; there was no one in the process of whatever you can be in the process of. I was very relieved.

4th November - Another visit to the midwife. The bump is getting much bigger. (Are you sure there is only one?) We heard the heartbeat, and again it is very strong and clear. The weight... well, the less said about that the better. Getting around is proving to be rather more of a struggle, but I am benefiting from not being at work. I can potter around the house during the morning and rest/sleep during the afternoon and try to stay awake when Ian is home in the evening.

The hall, stairs and landing are virtually finished and then we'll do the nursery. The midwife tells me I must rest more. But I can't rest – I want to be active and do things!

10th November - Today I had a hair appointment and met a friend in town for lunch. I'm really starting to enjoy not working. The sun was shining and I always feel great after having my hair done. Lunch was taken at a luxurious pace and I didn't have to dash anywhere, so I strolled around Mothercare and the Early Learning Centre looking at things I would like for the nursery, I never realised I would want so much – I'd better not tell Ian, he'd have a fit! I got the mid-morning and mid-afternoon trains/buses and this meant that I didn't have to struggle with standing on packed trains, this is really nice. While I was in town I saw some Aran wool on special offer so I bought some plus a pattern and started Ian's jumper, I can knit when he's out.

2nd December - The nursery is completed - I have been painting, plastering and fitted a dimmer switch, Ian has been papering. At Ian's parents the other evening his mum asked me if I was putting my feet up watching the soaps on day-time TV, I told her what I had actually been doing, she looked sort-of blank and then asked me if I wanted a cuppa, I don't think we were raised the same, we're certainly not on the same planet!

Yet another visit to the midwife. Things seem to be progressing rather well - fortunately. I read and re-read books on pregnancy and birth and learn all about eclampsia and pre-eclampsia, and fill in the "kick-chart" with almost religious regularity, I'm eating all the right things and trying to sleep. I've decided to try a TENS machine during the labour, it's drug free and doesn't cut out my other birth options, I think the only time I couldn't use it is if I go for a water birth. I don't fancy one of those in case there's too much mess, I'd probably die of embarrassment.

7th December - Experienced a VERY LARGE practice contraction and it scared me to bits. It was 10.30am in the morning and I had been doing a little gentle pottering around when **WHAM**, I was suddenly aware that in a handful of weeks this baby is due to make a personal appearance. I sat down to get over the shock and told Ian on the evening. I packed my case ready for hospital and we talked about the time when baby decides to arrive, Ian says he doesn't mind when it is as long as it's not during one of his TV programs! Why am I not surprised!

13th December - I experience some niggling pains, which disappear after a bath. This is becoming rather worrying. I'm not ready, but it appears that baby might be.

16th December - I talk to the midwife about what has been happening over the last couple of weeks, she checks everything and pronounces that all is well, but I MUST REST!!!

I've got more stretch marks. Oh great! These are across my tum, I've now got so many that when I've given birth I'll have a tummy with the attractive look of corrugated cardboard!

17th December - I visit the hospital where I am hoping to give birth (did I really say hoping?). It's very nice. It's very well laid out, rather like the local hospital we visited during the parent-craft course, all the same (frightening) equipment, the monitor, the bed, the stirrups, the baby machine should anything be wrong with the baby when it is born, it's all there, all sterilised, all ready. I asked questions and tried to be jovial, but that's just for show, on the inside I'm petrified. I told Ian and as always he thinks I'm making a fuss over nothing, he told me giving birth is like shelling peas as his mum had almost enough kids for a 5-a-side team. Hmmm not very supportive Ian.

19th December - A friend of mine visited and bought her baby along for a couple of hours. This was a lovely visit. But then she told me all about her labour and delivery, this is not what I needed to hear as a couple and their little baby came visiting the other day and told me of that labour too. Both labours can only be described as horror stories. Tales of emergency theatre, blood transfusions, forceps, stitches and all manner of frightening things. I'm not sure how to react when I hear these sort of things from friends who I know and trust not to invent stories.

21st December - I have an antenatal visit with the Doctor (we're into weekly visits now!) as the practice nurse had said I've got protein in my water sample. This proves not to be the case, phew, what a relief, I'm still having a normal pregnancy! So I suppose not being able to turn over in bed without sitting up, not being able to tie my shoe-laces, cut my own toe nails, climb the stairs without walking very slowly; all these things are perfectly normal, acceptable, expected and ok! And someone mentioned it's Christmas in a few days. Christmas! I can't plan for Christmas - I'm having a baby!

27th December - Christmas has been a bit of a tug-of-war with patience, nerves and all that goes with them. We obviously had to do the Christmas Day lunch at Ian's parents, but I wanted to rest (really!) instead I was on my feet ferrying food and plates from the kitchen to the table and afterwards I was helping with the washing up – hmmm not what I had hoped for with a table of about 10 sitting down for lunch, but as most of them were blokes it seems that's what they expect from women.

When we got home Ian had a major sulk when I told him I was exhausted and was going to bed. Boxing day Ian wanted to visit some friends, so I said he could visit them on his own, he was almost beside himself with rage, it seems we have to do everything together, and he's said he wants to visit Karl and Vicky soon, I'm not in favour of this with the due date looming ... I don't think he considers this much of an event – I suppose he thinks I'm making a fuss.

31st December - What should have been a short shopping trip ended up taking us out of the house for 4 hours, and it was bitterly cold. As we were coming back from shopping the car broke down. Fortunately, we were by a pub and were able to park, make a couple of phone calls, and wait for help to arrive – Ian won't join any of the rescue services because of the cost. Ian's dad came and hooked up a thick rope to give us a tow home, but as our car was being towed off the pub car park it sprang into life again (?) it took a few days to get it back to working order, this is not the sort of stress I need. What if...? The thought frightens me.

6th January - Another midwife appointment. Things such as sleeping and the like are getting beyond a joke. The heartburn is phenomenal, I've been given something to take by the Doctor and it's been re-named "The Gin Bottle" since I can't actually have a G & T. Sleep is something I long for (so is a G & T!), but it evades me. My tummy has developed even more stretch marks and baby is bumping around less due to running out of space. It feels as if the baby's bottom-end is tucked up tight under my bust line and the head is pressed well down in my uterus - I think I'm going to give birth to a giraffe! Plus, and this puzzles me, underneath the bump is very uncomfortable and gives me nasty sharp pains that make me wince, as if I'm held together with safety pins!

8th January - 8.30pm contractions started! Yes, here we go, here we go... I rang the hospital at 10pm and told them what is going on. They say "Ok, go have a bath, ring us later, or come in". I dutifully have a bath and the contractions stop. Now what do I do? I feel deflated and disappointed. I've actually had enough of carrying this baby around, I want something definite to happen - I think; so I took myself off to bed before Ian could tell me I was making a fuss.

10th January - The contractions have been on and off for a couple of days now and I've - almost - started to ignore them.

11th January - Still getting contractions but today they seem stronger.

9pm - finds me in bed reading about labour of all things. Ian is down stairs watching one of his favourite programs before doing his sandwiches for work tomorrow, he comes to bed at 10pm; I tell him of the contractions, he tells me to go to sleep.

11.15pm - I notice that I've been having contractions at about 15 minute intervals. I wake Ian and told him. We get up and rang the hospital, they said, "Come in when your contractions are 5 minutes apart, when you can't take it anymore or if your waters break." I put on the TENS machine and watched the clock go round. Well, it doesn't so much go round as lurch from one contraction to the next. I am overwhelmed by the pain!

!! NO ONE SAID IT WOULD HURT THIS MUCH !!

The TENS machine is rather good, if (for me) not quite relieving the pain but at distraction! I kept this up for as long as I could.

3.00am - the contractions are coming at about 7-minute intervals and we decide to go to the hospital. At this time of the night there is very little traffic on the roads.

In the car I'm holding on to the handle above the door and each time I experience a contraction I'm screaming **"MIND THE POT-HOLES"**. The drive is 15 minutes long; I am now getting a contraction every 5 minutes. It seems a very long drive to the hospital and Ian has chosen to take the back streets route - as if there'd be traffic jams at this time of day!

At hospital the midwife and Ian walk on ahead of me chatting like old friends and leave me clutching the door handle having another contraction! The nurse gets a wheelchair and wheels me inside, it doesn't help that the wheelchair has a flat tyre. She takes my blood pressure and the measuring thingy does not work – she blames everything on government cuts, and she prattles on and on. She then examines me and tells me that I'm 3cm dilated.

3CM! IS THAT ALL!?

This could be a long night! I have a shot of pethidine to calm me down, and as I float to the ceiling I sort of snooze the rest of the night away.

8am - I'm not handling the pain very well and have an epidural fitted by a very competent doctor, and for some reason I've got a cannula in my hand – it's not really painful but as time goes on it gets uncomfortable.

For me the epidural proves to be both good and not

good. Although it helps with some of the pain it does mean that I can't get off the bed as I'm linked up to a monitor, plus the epidural slows down the labour (something they did not tell me at parent-craft). Also, the pain relief does not fully take and some of my leg muscles suffer dreadfully, the nurses keep turning me to try to get the numbing to spread! Every time I have a contraction Ian has to tell me to breathe as I'm in a dreadful state and not coping at all.

4.30pm - in the afternoon, after a very long and laborious (!) day and after having had the epidural topped up I am exhausted and no longer able to think for myself, as well as having gone through a few nurses due to shift changes, (even having whispered in the ear of one midwife to admit how terrified I am), I then have a Sister come and examine me (how many more people are going to take a look?). She takes Ian outside and explains the choices, I can either have the epidural topped up again and have a forceps delivery (a normal thing apparently for an epidural labour as you can't actually push the baby out yourself due to not being able to feel anything - something else they didn't explain at parent-craft!), or I can have a hormone drip linked up to the cannula in my hand, this will 'bump up' my contractions and make them more 'productive'. Ian knew I had made a birth plan and that I didn't want a forceps delivery, so the epidural isn't topped up and I'm linked up to a hormone drip.

I asked the midwife how long it will be for it to take effect and she said a few minutes. The midwife then tells me she is going to burst my waters, I can't wait for this as I've read so much about it – apparently if your waters 'go' in some posh stores they send you a big bunch of flowers! But when the midwife burst my waters there was disappointingly only a cupful of water, certainly no more.

So, the pain-relieving epidural fades in to the evening sky and **WHAM** the pain of actually being in full labour hits me like an express train! I grabbed Ian's hand and nearly broke it! The birth progresses quickly and soon the baby is coming. But I can't actually push the baby out as I'm exhausted and the midwife says I will have to have an episiotomy (small cut) quite frankly at this stage she could have cut my head off to get the baby out! Also, the umbilical cord is around the baby's neck and pulling against my pushes, so the midwife cut the cord while the baby is still inside me; then the baby is born quite quickly and popped on my tummy. The midwife says 'congratulations you have a daughter'. My response is that I have a daughter and I smile, I no longer have heartburn and I rest back on the bed. Ian's response was a disappointed 'Oh' as he was convinced that he was such a fine specimen of a man that he was bound to produce a male heir. The midwife left us for a while to get acquainted with our daughter Anna, who is so much a cutie that I now believe in love at first sight, sadly she's not interested in being breast fed. I then hit the gas and air while I was stitched up, as not only the cut needs stitching but I also tore inside and out during delivery.

I went for a bath, and later when Anna and I were settled on the ward Ian went home to make phone calls, get himself a curry and a beer. The first visiting time the next day the whole of Ian's family turned up! It was a dreadful disaster as you are only allowed 2 or 3 people around the bed at any one time; but they are not a family that follows rules.

Anna and I spent a few days in hospital before going home. Getting home was a bit of a shock as Ian hadn't got anything ready for Anna and I had to make up the cot and do much more than I had planned. This was quite tiring and unexpected. It's amazing what triggers me into remembering the 2nd thoughts I had about not going through with the wedding, as well as the fors and against list! Ian went back to work the next day and Anna and I got on with our new life.

18th January - A midwife came and visited us at home to check on things. I was so pleased to see it was one I knew from parent-craft. She was very pleased with me and with Anna. I'm still not getting much sleep as Anna is feeding every 2 - 3 hours, plus I'm feeling very sore and have hit the painkillers hard. I'm also trying to get used to the fact that I'm a mum; it's a big responsibility, I've got a very strong sense of protection towards Anna, and I believe this started during the early part of the pregnancy.

Anna is bottle fed as we didn't get it together with breast-feeding, she was very drowsy when she was born due to the pethidine I'd had in the early hours of the morning going through my system into hers. While we were in hospital we tried for a couple of days to do the breastfeeding thing but she was having none of it and then started getting quite lethargic, she also turned a little jaundiced so the nurses put her under a UV light for a few hours and on the bottle she went, and she thrived!! I've been expressing my milk and putting it in a bottle for her, she has my milk first and then if she's still hungry she has formula milk, she loves both.

27th January - A lovely health visitor called Kirsty came today to check on things. The midwife had discharged us both yesterday as Anna's 'button' had dropped off (!) and everything is going well i.e. she is feeding and sleeping and the nappies are as nappies should be.

The visitors have slowed down - thank goodness, as there are some people who will ignore hints that you are tired, even if you are in your pj's!

30th January - The Parent-craft reunion. Along we went with Anna in her car seat, and she slept the whole time we were out. Well, she does. People look at us with sideways glances when we say, "yes she does cry" and "yes she does wake up to feed", they don't believe us.

I'm really looking forward to Spring, I've finished Ian's jumper and surprised him with it – he sort of likes it and tried it on, but he won't wear it as he says he can't get a jacket over it – I explained that he didn't need a jacket with an Aran jumper but he's a bit like a mule and won't be persuaded – so I wear it when I go out for a walk pushing Anna in her carry cot pram thingy; I tell her all about what we can see – the changing over of the birds flying in and out, the lakes and the fells – I am saddened Ian won't wear his jumper though because I put a lot of effort into it – ho hum, soldier on.

Ian had said I can take time off work to be a mum, however as the weeks go by it became obvious that his idea and my idea of time off don't seem to match, so a couple of months later I found myself back in full time work and Anna in nursery; I hated being separated from her. I hated the thought that the nursery staff were looking after my daughter, feeding her, playing with her, watching over her when she slept, I hated it every single day. I felt the pull of mother guilt as if an invisible umbilical cord still connected us.

Spring is here and Anna is thriving. She's such a bonny baby with a cute smile, and no matter what I dress her in, whether it be her Sunday best or her sloppy jo's she looks great. I'm certainly captivated by the overwhelming love and protection I feel for her, plus I think I'm ready for my next adventure.

www.ingramcontent.com/pod-product-compliance
Lightning Source LLC
Chambersburg PA
CBHW061101050726
47592CB00004B/1771